When
Marriage
Ends

RUSSELL J. BECKER

2731

Fortress Press **Philadelphia**

POCKET COUNSEL BOOKS

Copyright © 1971 by Fortress Press

Second Printing 1975

Library of Congress Catalog Card Number 74-152366
ISBN 0-8006-1102-0

5135D75   Printed in the United States of America   1-1102

Series

Introduction

Pocket Counsel Books are intended to help people with problems in a specific way. Problems may arise in connection with family life, marriage, grief, alcoholism, drugs or death. In addressing themselves to these and similar problems, the authors have made every effort to speak in language free from technical vocabulary.

Because these books are not only nontechnical but also brief, they offer a good start in helping people with specific problems. Face-to-face conversation between counselor and counselee is a necessary part of the help the authors envision through these books. The books are not a substitute for person-to-person counseling: they supplement counseling.

As the reader gets into a book dealing with his concerns, he will discover that the author aims at opening up areas of inquiry for further reflection. Thus through what is being read that which needs to be said and spoken out loud may come to the surface in dialog with the counselor. In "working through" a given problem in this personal way, help may come.

WILLIAM E. HULME
General Editor

Contents

Preface

This book has been written as an aid to the person whose marriage has come to an end and who either has sought counseling or may be contemplating doing so. It does not have answers. On the contrary you might find it raises problems. It is for your own counseling work and for you to find the answers to these problems as they pertain to your life.

It is the assumption of this book that it is being written for the person whose marriage has come apart irreparably, hence the title, *When Marriage Ends*. The location of this book in a series permits it to have this single focus. It does not begin to suggest in any way the effort and desire of the author to help couples who may be having difficulties in their marriages before they fall apart.

A series of experiences which started in 1966 in the summer Single Parent Family Camp weeks of the Five Oaks Conference Center in Paris, Ontario, under the auspices of the United Church of Canada in Ontario has formed the backdrop to this volume. Since agreeing to write this three years ago, I have spent a year's sabbatical in Zurich studying the psychology of C. G. Jung. The time involved in gaining a grasp of analytic psychology has been vitally important to the shape which this volume finally took. Meanwhile each additional summer has added another exposure to over twenty different persons who were facing life "when marriage ends." I am indebted to these mothers who have shared with me their struggle to find themselves. I trust that only the persons involved may recognize themselves in the cases cited throughout the text. I hope, though, that each reader will find something of himself or herself on every page. More than that I wish for you the courage to wrest from the debris of your marriage a better understanding of yourself.

RUSSELL J. BECKER
July 15, 1970

1.

The
Agonizing
Reappraisal

Although newspapers and sociologists encourage one to think that divorce is becoming a commonplace of American life, one of the first discoveries you will make as a divorced person is that you are a strange woman or man. Former friends turn cool overnight—even those who you thought were your friends and not your spouse's particularly. They soon omit you from their social life. A woman will feel she has suddenly acquired some of the spirits of the Salem witches and is now a dangerous creature. No telling what subtle potions might be brewed by a woman who took the fateful step in ending her marriage, or received the crushing blow of having it terminated. A man in the same position is simply a Don Juan not to be trusted as capable of real commitments.

What does one do? Forget the past as a bad nightmare? Find the local Parents Without Partners group and start the dating game all over? Nurse one's bruises and incubate a bitterness which will poison your children's future? Try to go it alone as though nothing had happened?

Apart from these natural inclinations there is a constructive way of approaching divorce. We are not concerned with what might have been done to save the marriage. There are many things which fall in that category. But such belongs to the sphere of premarital and marital counseling. Assuming that the worst has come, how can one make the best of it? I am convinced that *postmarital counseling* is an unavoidable necessity. An "agonizing reappraisal" cannot be shunted aside. What went wrong? How did I fail? Is life worth living? Is there any future for me? What do I do now? How do I know I won't make the same mistake again? These questions thrust themselves into consciousness whenever we relax our guard. They are the proddings of our inner self urging upon us some greater self-understanding. Seeking out one's pastor for postmarital counseling is a first step toward "finding oneself."

But, you will argue, "I am not the disturbed individual. It was my husband (or wife) who ran off with another woman (or man)," or degraded himself with alcohol, or simply walked out. "He (She) is the one who is mixed up, not me."

Granting that there is an objective basis to some of these defenses, I must add that there is likely to be a heavy load of subjective self-righteousness involved as well. However, this subjective distortion of objective events is exceedingly difficult to catch. So let us pause a minute. One of the well-nigh invincible ways in which the conscious ego protects itself from criticism is involved here. When we are convinced that our emotional problems are due to an external circumstance we usually have some objective fragment of truth to point to. What we cannot see is the way in which we project onto that outward fragment some very strong feelings and interpretations of our own. We take a fragment of truth and make it a colossal fact. We overload the objective reality with all of our inner bruised feelings — seeking unwittingly to make ourselves look better to ourselves and others. This happens so smoothly we do not see our own subjective part in the process. We are convinced that we are reporting what happened "out there." In truth we are caught in a self-protective mechanism. A heavy proportion of what we think is "out there" (the unhappiness caused by a spouse's infidelity, cruelty, or spitefulness) is actually within ourselves. This is so difficult and painful to see that one simply cannot do this by himself.

If you have not spent more than your first hour with a counselor, I suspect more than a mild disbelief will rise within you here. If you have not even sought a counseling appointment I implore you not to close this book forthwith. Let us look at the whole situation this way: marriage is a relationship of two persons. The breakdown of a marriage which was freely entered upon by two persons must involve both parties *in some way*. Granted there is evidence that your spouse failed in very demonstrable and wretched ways to fulfill his or her side of the bargain, it takes two to break, fully as much as to make, a marriage. One of these two is yourself. There is a wisdom in the old Chinese observation that when we point a finger at someone else, three fingers point back at ourselves.

The first hurdle then is the acknowledgment that the failure of one's marriage is in some way one's own failure. One psychoanalyst has put this issue flatly in the title of a recent book: *Divorce Won't Help*.[1] The professional psychotherapist, the pastoral counselor, and the family counselor see too much evidence of the subtle intertwining of personality problems when family failure occurs to believe that "responsibility" in the legal sense is ever one-sided. Overt acts of infidelity and cruelty can be specified. What courts can never see are the subtle factors.

There are many arenas, including the sexual one, in which one may contribute to the collapse of a marital partnership. One woman used religion as the divisive wedge. Her own analysis, not too surprisingly, projected the problem outside as a matter of objective difference. "He wanted to go to bar rooms, and I went to church. He used bad language and kept the wrong company. I thought he would want to be better!" In the therapy group that she joined she complained about the way her husband had disparaged her. Before a handful of meetings had passed, the group found her own rigid moral pronouncements insufferably predictable and disparaging of everyone else. If only that ex-husband had met with some of those in the group who spent this week with his "religious" wife, he would have found sympathy beyond all reckoning. Instead of a love which suffers long and accepts, this woman had distorted her religious position into a pharisaical righteousness. What she could not see was the extent to which she was accusing her former husband of the very thing which was her own most

1. Edmund Bergler, *Divorce Won't Help* (New York: Hart, 1966).

3

disturbing fault: a constant disparaging-of-others attitude. The great temptation to marry someone with the hope of changing him has its "holier-than-thou" seeds of destruction for the marital relationship.

If one can admit that there is some shortcoming within himself, then the next step is to want to get help. Here many people who would otherwise be well on their way to the pastor's study get sidetracked. Some excuse themselves from this step by finding an external reason to avoid counseling.

An argument against going to a counselor which lies in the borderland between the external and the internal says, "What good does talking do?" Of course talking that is for the purpose of fooling others or oneself may not be very helpful. But talking with the intention of working through the emotional "hang-ups" in our lives is of the very essence of becoming one's true self. And talking for the purpose of greater self-understanding is the only truly human option available to us. Martin Buber has called the realm of dialog, the realm "between" man and man, the humanizing realm. Every mother sees this phenomenon unfold in the infant's coming to consciousness. It is the human interrelationship culminating in the mutual participation in language in which the miracle of conscious selfhood occurs. Little wonder then that it is the miracle of dialog which should unfold and reveal the new creature we are to be. In biblical terms it is through Christ that we come to be new creatures. Christ is understood as the Word of God spoken that men might come to a newness of life. The word between ordinary humans shares in the mystery of the Divine Word which bridges the realm of the divine and the human. Our human words build relationships and rebuild the world we see. And out of new combinations, new perspectives, come new ways of being. "What good does talking do?" Talking can lift us to the realm of a divine mystery wherein God's redemptive, re-creative work takes place.

The deeper obstacles. to seeking help even when we know we need someone to talk to arise from the enormous inward pressures to turn away from that which is painful. There is only so much hurt and suffering which any of us can endure without the mercy of denial and repression. When it still seems salvageable, we have some motivation to endure the great pain of misunderstanding in the marriage. After marriage ends, we can too easily persuade ourselves no great value exists to conterbalance the distress of rehashing the past. "Let's forget about the past and face the future," one divorcee announced in a group therapy setting. But then she revealed that she had landed in a mental hospital before discovering that she had to talk her way back to sanity. And she candidly added, "That talking takes about two years—then you can face the future." She made abundantly clear the fact that there is no way around one's personal history, its examination and reintegration after severe rupture has occurred. "That talking takes about two years" when the disturbance in oneself is very severe.

There is a positive which offsets the negatives in looking at the painful past. This is the prospect of a better, more sound self. For the male, this concern may not surface until he is about to enter a new marriage. At such a time, he wants to think through what he is doing and make sure that he is not just the same problem again. For the woman, there is a more urgent issue when children are present. Just the continued functioning as a parent poses the question of adequacy. Leaving thought of any remarriage aside for the moment, the responsibility of child-rearing goes on. If the question of a better self-understanding can be ignored when it is for one's own benefit, it cannot be ignored when the welfare of one's children is taken into account. The ways of inflicting damage upon the children of a divorce are endless. The son who looks just like his father can easily be made to bear the weight of all that is felt and unexamined toward this now derelict parent. Within the close confines of the family, a daughter can be made to think all the negatives about men which the bitter wife may feel. The strains of being both father and mother to one's children cannot help but be insufferable and lead to disagreeable irritability. Even while it is true that the elimination of the emotional tension of a deteriorating marriage may be a relief, there are other tensions which fill the empty house. Tensions and anxieties are legion.

There is a third aspect of the movement toward a counselor which cannot be forgotten. It is implied in what we have said thus far. But it needs to be made explicit. The initiative and the responsibility for change and greater self-understanding is your own. Counselors do not make you different. They offer an opportunity for you to find out something about yourself. Not only is your own determination to seek help important, but the continuing concern to find out about yourself is central to the counseling relationship.

The process of change and self-discovery comes about when we disclose ourselves to someone else. Telling a trusted person about oneself sets in motion a loosening of the hard and fixed boundaries of the conscious self. Things which lie outside of awareness can come into view when the primary action of the conscious self is one of giving itself away. Not only do we remove the masks which keep others from knowing who we really are, we also take away the filters which keep us from knowing things about ourselves that might be uncomfortable or less than flattering. The biblical injunction, "whosoever would find his life, shall lose it" could not be closer to the truth. A sacrificial giving away of oneself through self-disclosure is the paradoxical route to self-discovery. Holding oneself in closely, playing one's cards close to the chest, is an apparent keeping of oneself. But it entails the loss of the fuller self which each person may be. Not simply the present consciousness, but the fringes of awareness and the depths of the more unconscious aspects of one's personality all are needed to effect a workable and fuller understanding of oneself. Without these unknowns brought to awareness we continue to be buffeted about by forces and factors which seem external but which are in fact simply aspects of ourselves left out of the whole picture.

We have traced three steps which need to be taken in the post-marital situation: (1) You need to face the fact that you are involved in the failure of a marriage. Regardless of all the other external circumstances, there is still your own responsibility for your own *responses* which cannot be eliminated from the marital picture. (2) You must recognize that dealing with your own responsibility means getting help from someone who is prepared to be of assistance in personal matters. Availing yourself of a counselor's help means taking the bit in the teeth. (3) Then pursuing the helping process means the self-directed response of finding out more about yourself through self-disclosure in a confidential relationship.

But, it might be asked, where does religious faith enter the picture? In the first place, religion ought not to be a smothering blanket helping us to hide from the guilt and pain of our own existence. After marriage ends, religion cannot make its contribution by reminders about the sacredness of the bonds of fidelity in the marital union. Religion cannot profitably make the already divorced person more conscious of his responsibility to work with his partner toward the realization of a marriage. Many doors are already closed. What is not closed is the question of one's own attitude toward life, both the past and the future. Even the disaster of a broken marriage can be met as a religious challenge. What does God seek from me now? What is the meaning of what is happening in my life? What is the purpose of so much suffering?

A purely naturalistic approach to the question of postmarital counseling could be limited to my wanting to find out what went wrong and what more of myself must be reckoned with. But the religious dimension of this counseling and of any life-situation is hinted at by the question: What divine purpose lies embedded in these events? The work of the prophets in the Old Testament revolved around this question. National disaster and natural calamity were the occasions for searching out God's ways which are higher than our ways. Or, in the story of Joseph and his brothers, the meaning of Joseph's surreptitious sale into slavery is put in terms of God's purposes. Speaking to his brothers, Joseph says, " . . . you meant it to me for evil, but God intended it for good" (Gen. 50:20). The religious issue we face after divorce is: What is the purpose of this turn of events? What does God intend in what has happened and in what lies ahead?

If you are content with the question of what went wrong you may easily be trapped in a simple interpretation of life as "nothing but" the working out of this instinct or that set of environmental circumstances. If you limit your views to "what more should I know about myself?" you are assuming that the individual self contains its own self-sufficient explanations of meaning and purpose. By raising the question of meaning and purpose explicitly—and from a divine perspective—we remind ourselves that our accountability is not to instincts or to ourselves but, ultimately, only to God.

It is hard enough in the midst of the humiliation and anguish of divorce to ask what happened and what was my part in it. It is an even greater test of faith to ask what purpose God intends in the midst of all this. Yet this is the religious issue in the midst of any life situation. Not, how do we justify ourselves to ourselves, but how do we find the hidden meaning in events which seem so bitter? Is there some admonition of the Lord written into what has happened? Is there a chastening love which will not let us go? Are there indeed everlasting arms underneath? Standing in the grace of God is not abrogated by crisis and hardship. It may even be made plainer if we but permit ourselves to think upon the cross-filled way in which God chose to make himself known in his fullness to men.

An agonizing reappraisal cannot safely be ignored by the persons who have compounded a divorce. This reappraisal requires not only seeking some counseling help but also turning toward the adversity and asking its purpose. In this way we grow. As the saints know, it is in the dark night struggles of the soul that God steels us for the stress of life.

2.

Divorce's
Grief
Work

There is a great deal written about the period of engagement and early adjustment in marriage. Some attention is paid to the marital readjustment which the arrival of children brings. But until recently little attention has been given to the emotional crisis which divorce entails. To be sure there are ominous sounds from many quarters indicating that difficulties are in store for the divorced person. The economic headaches and worries over the welfare of children are important concerns. But the first issue in the postmarital life is the emotional disengagement from one's former partner.

Because there usually has been a great deal of emotional turmoil leading up to a divorce, it is not surprising that one would expect being alone again to be peaceful. And relative to the quarrelsome or anxious last days of a marriage, the first weeks of being alone again may seem like a blessed relief. However, the cessation of hostilities does not usher in peace between former mates any more than between nations. There is work to be done if one is to achieve some inner calm and detachment from one's marriage partner. It is quite similar to the "grief work" which must be entered upon when death takes a partner. What do we mean by the phrase "grief work"? It is the process of looking at one's feelings in relation to an important loss. Whether they are feelings of anger, guilt, anguish, hurt, loneliness, disbelief, it does not matter. They are the feelings occasioned by the loss.

Divorce is a kind of death. The hopes and dreams of marital bliss perish. The relationship with someone you have loved and given yourself to comes to a halt. If the relationship had already died in the marriage then the divorce is a kind of burial ceremony. If the rupture was unexpected and disappointing, then the emotional loss divorce brings is every bit the same as that which death brings. Except death is final. And because your former mate still exists, you may deny for a while that an emotional detachment from him is necessary. Or because you may feel "good riddance" you may not see that there is grief work to do nonetheless. Regardless of whether your emotional feelings toward a partner are positive or negative, the cutting off of an opportunity to interact with your spouse is a loss that must be compared to death.

The denial that there is some important work to be done with their feelings is the most frequent characteristic of divorced people I have seen. In the bereavement situation, the attempts at the denial of loss and hurt are varied. In the divorce situation, the denial process usually takes the form of not wanting to talk about what is over and done. Unfortunately there is no more escape from feeling-involvements with persons through turning away from them than through their dying. A rising anger or disgust or longing toward one's former mate creeps in upon the ex-wife or ex-husband at unexpected points. There is no escape from having it out with one's feelings about the absent partner. This becomes the initial issue of postmarital counseling.

The tendency to think of the divorced woman with children and the widow with children as being in the same circumstance has been accentuated by the Parents Without Partners movement and by any "single-parent" grouping in church or community. In making the analogy between the emotional detachment process for divorced persons and the grief work of the bereaved, I might be easily misunderstood as lumping these two groups together. In actuality their problems are more dissimilar than alike. And when we compare the "grief-work" process of the divorced, some of these differences become readily apparent. The widow is permitted to grieve. Sometimes well-meaning friends block the process by distracting conversation or false cheeriness. More typically they feel their own sorrow and permit the widow to speak of hers. The funeral, unlike the divorce proceedings, is a social occasion in which the support of many persons is offered to the bereaved person's feelings. Afterward some period of mourning is socially accepted. Pastors know how to come to the bereaved and they open doors to the working-through of the grief reaction. For the divorced, no social support or social occasion softens the blow. Inner distress, anguish, loss, bitterness, envy, hostility are bottled up. Society provides no ready-made outlet for such feelings. The divorced person faces a societal "conspiracy of denial" regarding inner reactions. Given the natural inclination of the individual to put the past out of mind, society's disinclination to be emotionally supportive leaves divorced people in a psychic limbo.

The need to talk with someone in an honest self-disclosing way means the divorced person should seek out his pastor or take advantage of any offer he makes to be of help. The initial stages of the talking-out process resemble grief work. In the loss of a partner many feelings arise. There is no single pattern because the circumstances of each individual's life vary. But whatever the feelings are they need to be expressed and lifted to awareness so that their existence can be taken into account in future actions. Unexpressed, such feelings live a half-life in the shadows, always ready to intrude and disturb the process of living.

Disengagement after marriage takes time and talking fully as much as engagement before marriage does. You are not over and done with the investment of yourself in someone else just because you are no longer in his physical presence. In fact the feeling of anger and resentment toward your former spouse is a sure indicator that you are emotionally tied to that person. Hatred is just as much of a feeling-investment in somebody else as love. A reaction against another means that you are still tied to that

11

other person in very strong ways. The opposite of love is not hatred but detachment. Achieving some measure of detachment with respect to a former spouse is a prerequisite to peace with yourself.

When the divorced individuals have talked through the divorce so that there is a common agreement and decision, they provide for each other the kind of talking disengagement which enables each to turn away from the other on a reasonable basis. Such "rational" disengagement is probably quite rare. Although the statistics of Goode's study of divorce indicate that about half of those who get a divorce were actually separated before the divorce was secured, they also show that only a limited number of those interviewed had *many* discussions about the divorce prior to the separation (16%).[1] The other ways in which the break occurs that Goode calls "one-sided divorce," "drifting separation," and "delayed separation" all emphasize the likelihood that real disengagement talk between the two principals has not occurred. The overwhelming majority of divorced persons have "few" or "no" face-to-face discussions about the details of a divorce (68%).

The fact is that divorcees some months and years after the divorce took place welcomed the chance to talk about the circumstances of their marriage and divorce with a research interviewer. This shows us another aspect of the grief-work problem in divorce. This is the phenomenon of "delayed grief" found in the bereavement situation. It has its parallel in divorce. Feelings unexpressed about a critical circumstance in one's life do not dissipate by themselves. They are exceedingly tenacious. They come to life months and years after the event with a vividness which is astonishing. They surprise the person who holds these feelings fully as much as the one who listens to them. This is because the reactions to a traumatic event are strong. We are wrenched by them. Only by talking them out do we put ourselves in order again. The conscious self gains perspective and orientation for itself by looking at what happened. The absence of supportive help from others at the time

1. William J. Goode, *Women in Divorce* (New York: Free Press, 1965), p. 158.

of the crisis of a marital breakdown makes it most probable that "delayed grief work" will be the form in which help comes to the divorced person. Talking about the circumstances of the marriage, its disruption, and the subsequent events provides the needed strength for going ahead in life.

The feelings that were present at the time of the divorce are preserved almost as if in a deep freezer. A considerable amount of room temperature is needed to help frozen feelings thaw and change. The warm acceptance of a counseling relationship is the avenue by which this transformation occurs. Consider one divorcee who thought she had talked things through with friends. She discovered to her surprise that her inner feelings were still very vivid and unchanged. Although hers was a "one-sided divorce" in which she had left her husband and although she thought she was over and done with him, her affection for him was still quite real. When Mrs. G. first described the circumstances of her leaving her husband it sounded as though she were very much in control. "I knew I hurt him, but I didn't feel any great hurt. What disappointed me were all the ways he failed to be a good father and good provider and good husband before." Later Mrs. G., who was participating in a therapy group doing its postmarital "grief-work," burst out with an attempt to stop the discussion: "This is making me sad. I want to forget it all. For the first two years you have to talk about it, but then you want to just forget it." What her own sadness betokened was the extent to which she was still emotionally committed to her "rejected" husband. The apparent distancing of herself from him in dismay and disappointment over his inadequacies only masked the underlying hope that he would change. She was no further from him in divorce than in sharing his bed. She only thought she was. The hope that he would change so that the marriage could be resumed burned brightly. Her sadness gave her away. Later when she talked about why she had married him, it became apparent why she had divorced him and why she was still attached to him. In her words, "You want to change him. You marry him thinking you can change him." And she divorced him thinking she could change him. Neither of these facts had been seen until real listening occurred which pieced together her "sadness" in the group's discussion with her reasons for marriage and divorce. Though years had elapsed since her divorce, her feelings persisted much as they were at that time. Only in this therapy group could she see the extent of her attachment.

But in this case the extent of that attachment had an unrealistic factor in it too. Her marriage with the hope of changing her husband (like her divorce) was not predicated upon a genuine acceptance of this man. Her love was a conditional love. When she saw this she came to the more intrinsic problem of her self. Commenting upon herself in the second person, Mrs. G. said: "You send him to look for affection and understanding somewhere else. Why don't you give it to him?" Mrs. G.'s "grief work" enabled her to ask the big question of herself: "What am I doing when I don't really love and accept this man? Is there something in me which prevents me from being the kind of wholehearted loving person I would want to be?" The grief work delayed means that the exploration of more basic issues of the self are delayed too. But grief work is the starting point.

As we have seen "grief work" is the process of looking at one's feelings in relation to an important loss. (In Mrs. G.'s case the feelings of indifference were what she first expressed.) Expression of feelings regarding the lost spouse permits one to "take in" the loss. (Mrs. G. discovered her persisting attachment to the hope of changing her husband.) Suppression of feelings denies that any loss had occurred. (Until Mrs. G. saw how she wanted her husband to change, she could not know the loss she had suffered in her apparent indifference.) Acknowledging a change in reality depends upon allowing oneself to experience what has happened. Only in this way is the reality of the loss acknowledged. However, the analogy of divorce with widowhood breaks down on the issue of finality.

The finality of death makes grief work imperative. The continued existence and occasional contact with a divorced spouse lessens the likelihood that the equally necessary "grief work" will be done. The lingering hope of reconciliation which is felt by about one divorcee in seven[2] is a further obstacle to the acknowledgment of the reality of the loss and the changes it entails.

Even if there is a pulsing hope of remarriage, the provisional finality of the divorce needs to be reckoned with as a major change in the circumstances of life. Articulating the major upheaval of feelings which accompanies this change is the means whereby its reality is absorbed. Then a person is prepared to look at the larger issue of the internal self and its neurotic conflicts. This was the point at which Mrs. G. had arrived in her initial counseling work. So too with Mrs. E. In her grief-work stage, Mrs. E. expressed the hurt feelings of a one-sided divorce which had been initiated by her husband going off with another woman. Her anger boiled up at one point in group therapy with an observation intended to challenge all marriage counselors: "When there's another woman, you don't get a chance to go to a counselor." The distress over her changed status showed through when she complained about the neighbor's suspicious peering at any male family friend who might come to the door—however innocently. The pressure upon the children of a confusing triangle was expressed in terms of the children's not knowing "which woman their father belongs to." Only after these and several more exasperated remarks over the changed circumstance of her life were out could she seek individual counseling for herself. Now she was ready to acknowledge that the divorce had occurred and that she had effectively though unwittingly pushed her husband into the arms of another woman by her failure in making an effective sexual adjustment. At this level she was no longer concerned to storm and rant about the hurt and hardship of the marriage rupture. Now, she was prepared to do the serious work of self-exploration of her own conflicts and prudery about the physical side of marriage. With grief work done, the divorced person is ready to make the more searching explorations that are in order.

2. Ibid., p. 293.

Some disengagement from the entangled feeling-relationship with one's former spouse is necessary for future well-being. Painful as it may seem, the avenue toward this is "rehashing" the past, talking about what has happened to the marriage and what it's like to be divorced. This opening of old wounds makes for healing. Sealing these wounds over as though they did not hurt makes them festering sores for the future. Beneath the superficial wounds of divorce and the change in status it entails, there is one deeper blow which has been struck to one's self-esteem. This too must not be ignored. We shall look at this next as the progression of issues in postmarriage counseling unfolds.

3.

Adding
Insult to
Injury

However disruptive a marital breakup may be, the hurt which is felt more deeply than any other is the wound to one's pride. Economic dislocation may be serious. The wife will find herself headed into the labor force in nearly every instance after a marriage collapses even though this may not have been necessary before. Becoming a social pariah is painful enough. But here too one can take initiatives to meet new people. Family adjustments requiring both fathering and mothering where previously only a single parental role was demanded seem quite a burden. But adaptations are possible. In every instance where a broken marriage presents new problems, one is surprised at the resiliency of people, especially of the woman who finds so many changes to her life come with the collapse of her marriage. But one problem she faces cannot be eased simply by making a frontal attack. The ego-insult of having "failed" in marriage does not go away even after economic, social, and parental adaptations have been negotiated.

The problem of ego-insult is greater for the woman than for the man, so let me speak to the woman primarily. The male identification with a job which could prompt many men to take their lives in the Great Depression is the counterpart to the ego-insult which divorce delivers to women. Our society structures a greater share of the male's identity into his vocation and a greater share of female identity into her marriage. The woman forgoes her own name in entering marriage. How could we make it any clearer that her "all" is being put into this contract. Regardless of the reasons for the marriage dissolution, divorce tells a woman that she is a failure in society's eyes.

The man seems to walk away unscathed. Perhaps this is why the financial burdens the former husband faces with an earlier marriage continue to be so heavy. He pays with some of the income from his ego-strengthening work for some of the ego-loss which unavoidably falls upon the woman. Even when the woman herself has a job and a seemingly comparable social reward from it, she experiences the subtle social judgment of having failed in her vitally important social role in marriage.

There are some cushions. When it is a husband's alcoholism that underlies the marital breakdown, the failure seems not to be so obviously the wife's own (although a mate's part in alcoholism cannot be ignored). When personal inadequacies of the husband are such that he could not face and carry the mounting responsibilities of a family, the failure is not so much in the wife's character as in her having loved so blindly.

There are some severe jolts. Mrs. E. could not escape a sense of humiliation when she was jilted for another woman because she had also to reckon with the fact that her former husband was so sexually immature, even to being a Peeping Tom. Although sympathy came her way for having been left in her suburban bungalow while her husband went off to marry his secretary, she knew more than had become public knowledge. Early in their marriage, she had helped him cover up a Peeping Tom incident. She had tried to pretend it had not happened. The insult to her ego which had been present all along in the marriage had been masked. With her husband's sudden departure, she could no longer pretend that she had even the appearance of a marriage to shore herself up in her own eyes. For Mrs. E. the work of self-discovery beyond her grief-work period entailed the arduous task of understanding what had led her into this marriage in the first place. It was not easy as she put it, "for a grown woman of thirty-eight to admit that she was herself sexually as naïve as a twelve-year-old." Growing up to the point of realizing her own immaturities in the sexual sphere enabled her to move beyond the insult both of failing in her marriage and of having not chosen a sexually mature husband.

For some the failure felt in marital breakdown seems only to underscore how handicapped they were to begin with. Here I have in mind those people who enter marriage with two strikes against them—those who are themselves the children of divorce. One such person could articulate well the problem. The hurt felt after a marriage failure was the same as had been felt through earlier years in family failure. It came out as the feeling, "no one has ever loved me." Her mother busy entertaining a procession of men in her bedroom certainly did not convince Mrs. N. when she was a child that she was being loved and wanted. Her alcoholic father who made a pass at his own daughter didn't convince her of her lovability. The immaturities she brought into her marriage set the stage for a neurotic choice and a fantastic hoping that now someone would really love her. But she managed to marry someone so weak that he could not stand up to her compulsive testing of whether "no one loved her." She was prepared to tear everyone and everything to shreds with her brilliant and incisive mind.

Not until she had come upon a counselor who would not let her tear him apart and who would not cease to respect her either did she see the folly of her own testing-tearing-people-apart behavior. Only then did she see that her current ripsaw actions were primarily a means of proving her "no one loves me" thesis. From this she entered upon the long journey of personal psychotherapy until she found the shreds of self that she could respect. And then she found the first glimmers of acceptance of the goodwill and affection others were ready to accord her. The severe crippling of her own broken home and the inadequate mothering she had received had stacked the deck against any fair deal in her own marriage.

The sense of being a failure because of divorce does not need a chastening environment in which to flourish. It comes from the part of a woman which makes marriage so much a part of her own identity that she cannot avoid feeling inadequate and in the wrong when the marriage ends. What I have said in Chapter 1 regarding the need for a personal reappraisal when marriage ends, carries the implication of finding out what went wrong in oneself. I would not want to give the impression at this point, therefore, that the experience of ego-insult is simply a negative result of a collapsed marriage. It may be the necessary pain which drives one to the doctor. Without the prod within telling us we have failed, we might not be willing to search for our own flaws and the contributions they have made to the failure of the marriage. The ego-insult may be the fever that indicates there is real inner conflict. Something we have done (a marriage) has failed and we feel responsible for the failure in some way or the insult would not be so great. Thus the sense of ego-insult may be the handmaiden who guides us into counseling. There is after all something in need of more attention and understanding.

It is most difficult to accept the idea of having contributed to the marital failure when the cause of the sense of insult is another woman who has taken "my place." For the woman facing a divorce which her husband wants, there is usually another woman in the picture. On rare occasions the situation is reversed. But the pressures of a society in which the work-world of the male and that of the home front are separated to the extent we know them to be are all in the direction of placing the male in the company of other women— usually secretaries. The male does not go searching consciously. He usually has unconscious problems which may be unresolved and which marriage itself does not solve. The point is that any failure on either side to grow up within the marriage puts the male in the vulnerable position of avoiding his responsibility to mature by escaping to another choice of a mate.

That second and third marriages for males seem to work out is not to be taken as a sign of superior male ability in facing the inward growth issue so much as their running out of both libido and cash by the time they have worked themselves in and out of more than one marriage. (Male vulnerability to being lured away to another partner will be elucidated in Chapter 5.) Needless to say, many males do face themselves in extensive counseling work and surmount the growth problems that resulted from marriage failure; but more often other kinds of problems drive the male into counseling than marital failure alone.

To the abandoned wife, it appears that the wandering male has been snared by an unprincipled rival and she has lost again. Again? Yes, there is hardly a person who traverses adolescence without some experience of having loved and lost. The hurt pride that once was healed by rebounding into another's arms needs to be watched carefully. The temptation to prove one's desirability and worth by finding another male companion quickly should not be treated as a trifling impulse. We all need to be loved and wanted. And when we are spurned by one we have looked to for our emotional undergirding the need to be loved is all the stronger. In the alchemy of the soul sometimes the marriages of hurt egos prove as durable as any other. Very often, though, they leave out of view some dimension of mismatch that is based on important needs of one or the other partners which are temporarily submerged by the need to heal the wounded heart.

Mrs. L. was one whose counseling helped her to see just this set of dynamics. Not only had she the ego-insult of a marriage which failed, but like so many she had two children whom she wanted to experience a kind and loving father. When she found herself in a church camp setting in which a handsome man of her years was serving as a lifeguard, it was "love at first sight." Walks together, time together, being with each other at the community meals became imperative. The community, which was made up of single-parent families entirely, could not help allowing this new pairing to take place, but it muttered to itself that it was not right. After a year had elapsed and with it many months of a common-law relationship, Mrs. L. sought counseling help to understand herself. Now she had the common-law months of relationship to consider. Here she had discovered that this handsome hero who was gentle with her children and "everything she wanted" a year earlier was himself just a little boy who had left his first marriage to return to his mother and would someday do the same to her. Her great need for a loving relationship with a male struck him as a wonderful mothering quality to which he readily attached himself. Her counseling discoveries were almost "marital counseling" because of the common-law live-in arrangement of the preceding six or eight months.

She discovered through a dream how clearly mistaken had been her quick grasping of this strong and handsome-appearing male. This is her dream:

> "Bob appears in the dream on the kitchen floor face down. I pick him up and he is a two-dimensional figure—like a cutout doll—with eyes closed. He slides down to the floor inert."

Her associations with the dream: Bob is unresponsive about every thing. When she asks if he likes a meal, he may say, "No." "Do you like sex?" His response, "Oh yah," very mildly. The lack of responsiveness from her newfound second partner is just like the "lifelessness" of her father in her growing years. She looked to her father for approval and never got it. She now saw that Bob was coming on just as inertly as her father had. She said she would like to grab Bob by the neck and shake him alive. The paper doll who was lifeless on the kitchen floor in the dream was the unresponsive male whom she discovered after the sudden romance had settled into cohabitation. While a male to replace the husband who ran off with another woman soothed a hurt ego, he was no real help to other important needs. Mrs. L. gained the courage to break off this ill-fated match before it became another legally complicated and emotionally disturbing tie. Without counseling she would have been locked in the repetition of a childhood pattern between herself and her father with its simmering pot of anger for herself.

Divorce hurts a woman's pride. Perhaps it does so purposely to help her find a better footing for her own existence. There are far greater problems than having to suffer the deflation of the image which one has of oneself. Not knowing who or what one really is seems to be the greater danger in living.

In her last work the psychiatrist Karen Horney[1] seemed to take the position that the problem which the neurotic faces primarily is one of surrendering an idealized image of himself. Coming to see and accept the "real self" as over against the fantasy-fringed idealized image of oneself is quite a battle. It requires of everyone who would win that battle some uncommon courage. And each of the persons whom I have seen work his way through that battle-field bears the character of the heroic which ever after stamps him as an unusual and unusually attractive person.

What better way to overcome the assault upon one's self-image than to work through the issues and questions of "who I really am" and to modify oneself into something new in the process? Perhaps for each of us the discovery of the promised "new creation" we will be in Christ (2 Cor. 5:17) comes only when we have borne the pain of his cross and the healing of his stripes.

Certainly a part of the pain of self-discovery is finding out how much we need to grow up.

1. Karen Horney, *Neurosis and Human Growth* (New York: W. W. Norton, 1951).

4.

The
Child-Self
Within

Suppose we assume that the reader is persuaded by what we have said thus far that there is a task of personal counseling which lies ahead. It is a task made clear by the failure of the persons who were engaged in a marriage. The marriage appears to be broken beyond reconciliation, or nearly so. Each party to the failure needs to engage now in self-discovery. An expert counselor is needed: one's minister or priest, a social worker, a family-agency counselor, a community mental-health counselor, a psychologist, or perhaps even a psychotherapeutically oriented psychiatrist. What is in store for the person who seeks help in better understanding himself?

One discovers there is an inner child-self who is still very much a part of one's adult life. This is another side of the same coin by which we discover that aspects of our parents' lives are still very much alive within ourselves. In the process of human development, the child identifies with and incorporates the parent. He becomes like one or the other or both of his parents long before he comes to adopt in adult life the role of a parent. Beneficial as this may be in some cases it is clearly a disaster in others. Many young people in their late teen-age years begin the work of sorting out what part of the parent will be preserved and what discarded. This kind of sifting and sorting can occur before marriage and still leave untouched the other side of the coin.

Marriage itself touches the child-self within. The intimacy and closeness of husband and wife revivifies the earlier parent-child relationship. But not only do we find that we bear aspects of a parent within—usually the same-sex parent—we also bear residues of the child-self who used to face and cope with that parent. Fixed within the individual as though they were circuits in a computer are ways of responding and reacting to the spouse as though his spouse were parent and himself the child again.

When the behavior we display in a marriage is clearly childish —a temper tantrum to have our own way, crying to gain sympathy, bullying, or teasing—we sometimes catch ourselves. Invariably such behavior strikes our mates as childish and they are rarely slow to point out infantile actions, especially when such actions are crowding their own life-space.

But there are more subtle layers within the child-self. Especially difficult is the surrender of the child-self which has been neither accepted nor wholly rejected. Rollo May's work with anxious persons[1] uncovered a problem which the middle-class, respectable parent creates when he discovers that children are a burden and a nuisance. Respectable parent figures cannot let themselves reject outright the children they have borne. But they may be oppressed and inadequate to the task of being parents. As a result they present conflicting signals to their children: from the middle-class morality comes the message to the child: "I will be good and decent to you, especially if you are good"; from the disturbed part of such a parent comes the message that "I wish I didn't have my life weighted down with you." The child hears the verbal protestation of good parents: "Everything I've done has been for you." "We've sacrificed for you!" "You'll never know what suffering I've endured." Hearing these messages the child feels that the real parental unhappiness is in being strapped with a child. Rollo May calls this a circumstance of "hypocritical rejection." The middle-class child facing hypocritical rejection spends a lifetime trying to do the one more thing which would make a

1. Rollo May, *The Meaning of Anxiety* (New York: W. W. Norton, 1950).

parent deliver the promised love and acceptance. It never comes; but he never stops thinking it will.

This kind of rejection by parents creates a damaged child-self. Mrs. N., whom we spoke about in Chapter 3, showed the signs of outright rejection in her adult child-self. For it was that child-self which was convinced that "no one ever loved me" and "no one would ever love me." The miserable treatment she had received at the hands of a prostitute mother and a no-good father left her with little expectation that somewhere or somehow her mother or father could really care for her if only she would do something extra nice. On the contrary she had to work through the burden of a residual child-self who was convinced "people are no damn good."

But Mrs. Z. is another story. Her parents were the good church-going variety. As an only child, her sole duty seems to have been that she be a good little girl and properly adorn the respectable self-image of her parents. It was perfectly clear to Mrs. Z. that she did not amount to much, but if she were pleasant enough, others would befriend her. So she stretched her smile across her cheeks for the same reason that a puppy-dog wags his tail—hoping for a friendly response from someone. Others could walk all over her and she kept asking only to be liked. When her own husband left her with two children, she returned to her parents' home and went to work.

Not until one day when her father required her to hand over the keys to the family car did she realize that she was really a burden to her parents and had always been so. This gave her the spirit to move out into a place of her own, but not enough to examine the child-self within who still hoped for some little crumb from Daddy and Mother.

Three successive years she attended a one-parent-family camp week and dutifully obeyed the promptings of her child-self: be a good little girl, smile pleasantly, and don't mind if others step on you. Not until nearly the last day of the third year of such camp behavior did the group and the leader catch her game plan. "I will be all right by myself. Others need not bother with me. I do not deserve group time or attention." She would be a good little girl and sit in the corner without speaking. The group insisted that she had more to her than that. Indeed she did.

She had an anger for a mother who had died only a few months previously—an anger born of the deep frustrations felt by a child whom that mother had never really loved or cared about. She had fear that now her father would need her and expect her to move back to his house to be his maid and cook. But she also had anger for a father who did not really care about his "sweet little girl." She felt anger for having been made into a show piece, a paper doll, a decoration of her parents' home. Anger because the tidiness of a living room meant more to them than she did. She felt anger for not having had the chance to be accepted for herself or even as the child who was frustrated in being boxed into such a neat little mold. Hypocritical parental rejection had put her in the neurotic bind of hoping that one more smile or one more obsequious act or one more good deed would win parental approval. But it never did. And she did not know that it was futile to try. Only when the group goaded and role-played the anger out of her did she realize that angry girls could be loved and lovable. Then the realization that she no longer had to pretend to be good in order to gain some elusive parental favor, freed her to grow beyond her child-self. The good little girl whom she presented over three succeeding years to this group could be abandoned. A decent, likable adult with feelings, and anger at times, could take that child's place in her life. When this happened, the lines of the good-girl-smiles on her face changed into a peaceful countenance assured that "somebody I care about cares about me— warts, angers, and all."

It is not easy to reveal your child-self and give it away. The fact is that you do not see it yourself. But you can believe it is there. No one grows to maturity without passing through childhood and experiencing some kind of mothering. No one therefore is able to avoid some imprinting of the emotional responses the child feels are required in response to the particular emotional needs of the mother. There is therefore a child-self inside every individual as his particular hang-up. C. G. Jung used the term "complex" for this feature of human development. Rather than assume that there was one special complex that every human experiences, he was prepared to believe that every child's first crucial patterns of attachment to parental forces constituted his own unique lifelong "complex." For some, but not all, this complex might well be the "Oedipal" complex. For others like Mrs. Z. it is the good-little-girl complex where a particularly censorious or critical mother seems only to be calm and decent when the child is "pleasing" her. For Mrs. N. it was the hostile "get-lost" complex in which the child knows the parent really has no positive feeling for her. But the opposite parental attitude can be just as complicating for all future relationships. I have seen the child who was carried around on worshipful cushions who had to work through her "fairy-princess" complex. Such a complex expects of a husband a prince-consort role, which few men happen to have as their complex.

A complex is not something that one eradicates by counseling. Hopefully, and at best, a complex is something that one discovers as the child-self within. When discovered, the child-self does not dissolve and disappear. Some aspect of our child-self remains with us throughout our life. The reason is that the complex has the function of attaching us to life itself. Hence the elimination of our complex would be the cutting of the connections to that which makes us human. Coming to know one's own complex means that one can modify its intensity as an inner compulsion. But one should not expect the basic child-self or complex ever to disappear.

One seeks counseling therefore not to "cure" one's neuroses but, rather, to learn to live with them and to turn the suffering they cause to some good purpose. Awareness of one's complex should lead to respect for its tenacity, but the ability to counterbalance or discount only in part the distortions in living it causes.

Sometimes the discovery of the child-self may lead to eruptions. Here are two situations of this type in which it can be said that personal counseling led to divorce itself. In one, the case of Mrs. Y., the counseling which the wife received at a family counseling agency upset the neurotic equilibrium within the marriage itself. The husband reacted by finding someone else whose neurosis complemented his own the way his wife's precounseling hang-up had. He sought and obtained a divorce. In the other case, that of Mrs. X., the husband himself went for counseling and eventually the divorce was mutually agreed upon.

The counseling that Mrs. Y. received led her to conclude that an inadequate sexual adjustment with her husband was no longer tolerable. The child-self who inwardly thought sex was bad had dutifully accepted her husband's avoidance of sex. But the husband, a child of divorce, had developed an elaborate attachment to his mother, which the mother had carefully cultivated. One brother had managed to remain unmarried until forty years of age and then could manage only a single year of marriage before he returned to mother. The other son, the husband of Mrs. Y., had spent twenty years in marriage, but his sexual confusions had not been challenged by any strenuous interest or demand on the part of Mrs. Y. When she discovered through counseling that it was her inner child-self (convinced of sex as an evil) which had restrained her interest in and response to her husband sexually, she became upset with herself. Not recognizing how much her child-self restraints had dovetailed with her husband's inability to extricate sex from some incestuous complex, she started demanding more sexual attention. She was not willing to let her puritanical child-self keep her a frustrated female any longer. Her new aggressive interest in sexual relations with her husband horrified his incestuous complex wherein sex and mother were somehow all tied together. He started back-pedaling from his new "sex-fiend" wife and landed in the waiting snare of his divorcee secretary. She had both a proven coldness and a need for marriage (to support herself and her two children) which might permit him to get back to the state of a male being cared for without the sexual demands from his present "mothering" mate. By the time Mrs. Y. came to see me, it was too late to help her retrieve the effect of her over-reaction upon her marriage.

Had Mrs. Y. shown a little more respect for her own complex which, after all, had bound her to a particular man and marriage for over twenty years, she might have found some alternative to instant abandonment of the commands of her old inhibiting child-self. Counseling should help us to see the child-self of the past and to respect its tenacity. It should enable us to be less under its dictates, but we should realize that we never entirely escape its binding power to life. The proof of the power of Mrs. Y.'s old child-self was revealed in her "remorse" for having let loose some sexual aggressiveness. The bad consequence, the loss of her stable home, had only reinforced the old child-self's original position, namely, that sex is really bad.

A different course of events surrounded Mrs. X. Her counseling led her to see the dutiful-daughter, compliant child-self she had brought into marriage. For ten years she had lived the dutiful-child role with her husband so that his word was final. If he didn't like her artistic or musical interests, she obediently ignored her own desires. Only once, in the selection of a style of architecture for the house they built, did her interests count in a family decision. When she found herself being drawn to another man, she decided to seek counseling. There the little girl obedient to her parents was quickly seen. But she did not turn around and become a tiger, which would have frightened off her ruling-male husband quickly. She insisted that he too go for counseling as she was doing. He agreed that time for mutual adjustment seemed essential.

However, during the interval Mrs. X. began to discover that the artistic potential and interests she had were not casual or excludable. She began to paint and discovered that she had real talent. A veritable flood of painting was undammed. Now, the ten years of marriage in which her dutiful child-self had suppressed all this side of her life seemed more questionable. Her concern became one of wanting to protect her own gifts rather than to assault her domineering husband.

As time went on both parties agreed that the marriage was not the right mix for either of them. Mr. X. could say to Mrs. X., "You are just too complicated for me." Mrs. X could say of her husband, "He is not going to be satisfied with anyone other than a woman whose sole delight is in waiting on him." Both could see how much their marriage had been "arranged." Two socially prominent families had made the right connections. Each partner was discovering that there was more to a marriage than right connections and good outward appearance. And Mrs. X. was discovering that there was much more to herself than a nice-appearing, dutiful child. The movement toward divorce finally became a risk-taking for the more creative self which she could be. With the divorce accomplished she did not have an enormous residue of soul-searching. That had been accomplished before and during the divorcing process.

It seems ridiculous to suggest that grown men and women have a problem with the residual child-self. Until one has searched for it and discovered it, then ridiculous it must sound. Once one has tracked through the recesses of one's behavior with candor and honesty, it no longer is a matter of ridicule or dispute. It simply is a fact of living and a fact of every life.

5.

The
Unknown
Partner

"Why did you ever marry him (or her) in the first place?" is one of the most important questions the divorced person needs to ask. The answer will disclose another very important part of personality which too few of us ever see. Carl Gustav Jung has identified the aspects of the unconscious that have so much to do with our choice of a mate and how we live with him as the Anima (for a man) and the Animus (for a woman). The Anima or Animus is for each of us an unknown partner within.

This means that every person carries within himself an active set of reactions and characterizations which are organized as an opposite sex figure. This personification of the opposite sex is not something we see or know directly. It belongs to the part of our psychic endowment which is unconscious. But we should not disparage that which is unconscious. The powers of the unconscious can be far more determinative of our behavior than we are inclined to suppose. The self-conscious individual likes to think he runs his own life. The truth is that his life is influenced by the powers and energies of the unconscious constantly and is only occasionally modified by consciousness. Nowhere is this more true than in those unconscious aspects of ourselves which are constellated as the inner unknown partner.

The inner unknown partner rules our choice of mates. We respond with interest and delight in the person of the opposite sex which matches the characteristics of our inner unknown partner. Why does one person turn us on and another leave us cold? What prompts the specificity of our interests in one particular kind of person but not any other? What makes it love at first sight when we see one person, but not another? There must be something about us which sharply defines our interest in particular persons of the opposite sex. The fact is that we are drawn to that person whose manners, looks, speech, and reactions echo those of our own unknown partner within.

We choose as company, and are fascinated by, the person who is a suitable bearer of our projections of the unknown partner within. Everyone has a secret lover. When we choose a mate an important part of the secret is out. Strangely enough we do not see it even so. The biblical saga of Creation speaks about this inner partner whom we find in outward form. The Lord God caused a deep sleep to fall upon Adam. "And the rib which the Lord God had taken from the man he made into a woman. Then the man said: 'This at last is bone of my bones and flesh of my flesh; she shall be called Woman, because she was taken out of Man'" (Gen. 2:22-23).

Adam greets Eve and recognizes her as part of himself. Thus it ever was and thus it ever will be. The problem for contemporary man is that he has become skewed in his grasp of this biblical truth by his physical and scientific preoccupations. Only a psychology that ponders mythical and imaginal truths can recover for us the message. And the message of the Creation saga is that the opposite sex partner we meet and love is in truth the divine creation of a person who is a part of ourselves.

Further support for this understanding of the mating process is found in the words of Yahweh, "It is not good that man should be alone" (Gen. 2:18). The divine mystery in creation includes the plan for mating. Man should not be alone. A companion is an essential part of man's existence. But then it turns out that the companion for man is derived from the interior of man. What the Creation saga speaks of in physical terms is actually a psychological process. Certainly the hand of the divine is no less present in a psychological process than in a process described in physical terms. Man meets and recognizes woman as flesh of his flesh and bone of his bones because, in Jungian terms, it is his Anima who comes to him as a lover and mate. The unknown partner within appears as the woman who captures his fancy.

What a man does in choosing a partner is to recognize the divinely formed unknown partner within, his Anima, his soul-mate. All the romantic utterances of needing her and being unable to live without her are perfectly true according to analytic psychology. The Anima within fastens itself upon the appropriate outward woman and the man is enraptured by that particular woman. Such is the inner alchemy of mate selection. Why then doesn't everything turn out the way the fairy-tale ending goes: "They lived happily ever after"? There are a number of answers.

The Anima within may not be a Fairy Princess. The Animus within may not be a Prince Charming. Not every Adam has the benefit of the exclusive attention of God in the shaping of his Eve. Various encounters with mothering figures and significant others of the opposite sex share in the formation of the Anima. Fathers and their surrogates shape the Animus.

When Mrs. E., whom we spoke about in chapters 2 and 3, was asked why she married the man who turned out to be so immature in his own psychosexual development, her answer revealed the distorted nature of her Animus. She said she had chosen a weak male who permitted her to be in charge! This made her less than feminine herself and helped to emasculate further an already too delicate male. Very likely Mr. E. had an overly soft Anima derived in part from an overpowering mother. Each had chosen a partner who accentuated the weakness of his own sex-role identity. Mrs. E. came on too strong; Mr. E. too gently. When the Animus within the female works its way out in her own conscious and daily behavior, that woman is a caricature of a man. When the gentle, feminine Anima of a male works itself out to the surface in the behavior of the male, he becomes a caricature of a female. The strong and healthy Animus of Mrs. E. was hedged in by a father who took a subservient role to a dominating mother during the developmental years. Consequently nothing but a weak, battered Animus remained within. When Mrs. E. heard her own description of what kind of man she had chosen, she was chagrined. As her counseling proceeded the hard, tough-skinned masculinity of Mrs. E. began to subside from her own behavior. With this subsiding, her interest in a healthy, dominating, sexually aggressive male increased. The inner recovery of a healthier Animus prepared her for radically different male-companionship choices. Unless there had been the shock of having actually described the nature of the husband she had chosen, she would not have seen how repulsive her "lovely, Christianly active marriage" was.

It is important to describe for yourself the characteristics of the mate you did choose and see if you can stand the picture objectively. If not, then you know that there is work to be done. Only now the work is not a matter of "what's wrong with the partner." That kind of projection no longer succeeds. Now the problem is clearly a matter of your own self, your own battered Animus or Anima, your own misplaced sex emphases or desires.

In another case, that of Mrs. D., her answer to the question why she had chosen her no-good husband in the first place drove home to her how much she had undervalued herself. She stated that she wanted only a physically attractive male. For a highly intelligent woman to have held to that single condition meant only that she was radically shortchanging herself. When she found that her choice meant an aggressive sexual partner—which she liked—as well as a physically abusive male with few refinements of mind or character, she knew she was in an intolerable situation. When the physical abuse began to include her children, she gathered her children and ran. Only when she began to acknowledge her own intellectual and religious interests as a real part of her life could she begin to see something of what the better or healthy Animus of her life might be. Until Mrs. D. could say to a counselor and to herself that she had chosen a male for reasons of physical attraction alone, she could not help projectively accusing her former huband of having been a beast who was only interested in sex. The moment she verbalized her reason for choosing him, the accusations against his failure dropped from the picture.

Let me return to the question of why things do not work out "happily ever after" and approach it from a slightly different angle. Not only is there the matter of a distorted or damaged Anima resulting from childhood development, there is also the fact that the person we marry is a *person* and not just our inner unknown partner image. There are therefore four persons in every marriage. Perhaps six. There is the person I am and my Anima. There is the person of my wife and her Animus. There is also the person I consciously wish my wife to be—an entity somewhere between myself and my Anima. And there is the person my wife wishes I would be. Little wonder that every marriage is a very complex affair even without any intruder.

Faced with the fact that your partner is a real person and not just what you have unconsciously projected onto him of your own hidden inner soul-mate, marriage requires some adjusting. Somehow the reality of the other person needs to be loved as well as the image you hold of the other. Your image of the other comes from yourself. It is in truth a part of you. And when you fall in love with someone who evokes that image, you are falling in love with a part of yourself. This is enough to get us married. But it is not enough to keep us married. There is invariably a discrepancy between the projected Anima and the real-life woman. Acknowledging this discrepancy and embracing the woman as she is requires an enormous growth step.

The dynamics for the disruption of a marriage arise when we are unable to look beyond the projected or wished-for mate to take in the objective one who walks, talks, and sleeps beside us. When we are unable or unwilling to reconcile our inner image and the outer reality, the inner image becomes foot-loose. Even without our knowing it, the Anima or Animus takes off. We know it has landed when we find another person who fascinates us. The spark of our own soul is now kindling in another outward person and we find that all life now revolves around that other one.

Except in the case of the Don Juans of both sexes who are collecting bed partners to shore up their own image of themselves, the wandering Anima or Animus is seldom a casual matter. Jolted out of congruence with the marital partner, the Anima seeks another roosting place. When the disaffected partner finds a new person "who really understands me," he is prepared to make the same eternal pledge which he made once before. Everything else becomes rationalization and justification of the inexplicable rightness of the soul-mate one has found. Such is the power of the Anima/Animus to lead us around by the nose.

It need not be a fitful matter. The connections which the Anima or Animus lead us to are important. They are no less than some important part of ourselves. But there needs to be reflection, observation, consciousness, and consideration as well as connections with another person. Therefore the "objective" part of the partner we choose is important too. This requires some moving outside ourselves to the actual consideration of and caring for a different person. When we let the Anima or Animus lead us into the life of another and then turn away in disappointment because all is not as we had wished or fancied, the wandering journeys of the Anima or Animus can make us simpletons searching for the perfect mate. The grim truth is that staying with the mate the Anima or Animus chooses in the first instance could be the perfect solution if only we would recognize that marital partner for what he or she actually is. This, coupled with the soul-mate "halo effect" which surrounds our passionate choice, is enough to bring heaven on earth for anyone.

The virtue of marital bonds is that sometimes they hold us in one place long enough so that we do start to grow. We not only connect with another but we communicate with and consider another and thereby grow some more. The process of "hanging-in" with a particular mate means that we enlarge the range and quality of our Anima or Animus. This is all to the good.

When the answer one is able to make to the question of what attracted him to his mate in the first place turns out to be something which is not flattering to either, it is sure to be a negative or weak Anima that guided the choice. It should now be abundantly clear that the Anima (or Animus) can have both attractive and repulsive possibilities. The form of the Animus can range from the Fairy Princess to the Witch; the form of the Animus can vary from the Prince Charming to the Giant Monster.

Once a destructive or sickly inner unknown partner is discovered, one faces the problem of understanding what strands of developmental experience were woven into this misshapen form. Until this discovery is made, the power of the suspected Anima figure may be too easily discounted. Consciousness does not easily open a place to the hidden inner partner. That inner partner's realm is the unconscious. However much it may strive to gain a place in the sun, the attitude of the conscious ego is rarely open and hospitable to it. Therefore one requires many connecting lines to tie up awareness to the reality of unconscious aspects of personality.

If you are unconvinced about the reality of the Anima or the Animus, consider one additional matter. "The show is over but the melody lingers on." The formerly married person usually develops a generous animosity toward the rejected or rejecting mate. But at the same time, there is a residual soft spot in nearly every instance. Sometime when matters affecting the children require a meeting, the old flames begin to rise. What is there about this rejected or rejecting one which still doesn't "wash out of my hair"? It is of course the glove-close fit of soul to soul. Even where much vituperation, or abuse, or ego-insult has been borne, the unconscious partner within still meets itself in this one particular other. I listened with surprise to one man who had taken to referring to his former wife regularly in foul-mouthed expletives. For at the same time, he was on the verge of reconciliation every time they met. The Anima is not destroyed just because the exterior relationship has crumbled.

It takes quite a bit of work to appreciate that part of you which actively committed you to a mate who turned out to be a failure, a cad, a cheat, a bore, or worse. Until that part is reckoned with, the melody is apt to linger on. Residues of irrational response to the departed spouse will well up repeatedly. When at last you see that part of yourself which was responsibly involved in the ill-fated relationship, you have something which need never again be a surprise. This is not to say that you will never again feel tugs from this part of yourself. But once the forces which were hidden are acknowledged, they usually can be managed.

6.

The
Darker
Side

We have referred several times to Mrs. E. Let me mention her again from the perspective of the darker side of human nature. Mrs. E. was shocked because of her husband's sexual immaturities; his Peeping Tom activity which got him into trouble with the law was one example. Although it was true enough that he did have sexual immaturities, when she first felt the shock of his leaving her for another woman she could not see or admit the fact of her own sexual immaturities. After a year or more in which she had been receiving counseling help, she could remark with astonishment that she, a thirty-eight-year-old woman, did not have even an elementary-school-child's knowledge of her own sexual physiology. Only after divorce did she discover what a sexual climax was. But until she gained the perspective on herself which permitted her to describe herself as about twelve years old sexually, her anger and rage and feelings of humiliation due to her husband's unmentionable activity had to be seen to be believed. In the initial period after the collapse of her marriage, *he* was the heel; *he* was the sick one; *he* was the failure; *he* was the cause of her unhappiness; *he* was the one who needed a psychiatrist! She was the saint; she was the dutiful house-wife and mother; she was the one who had "forgiven" his first run-in with the law for voyeurism; she was the one who had stuck with him even when her family thought her foolish.

When the pot calls the kettle black it rarely sees itself. The psychological process is called "projection." It is the most difficult defensive maneuver to catch. Stated another way, projection is the most effective ego-defense any of us use. When we see the faults of others we are just observers. When we attack the faults of others we begin to think of ourselves as above such traits. This gives us a feeling of superiority and righteousness that is exquisite. But the truth is that our delight in attacking the faults of others betrays us. The more energetic we become in excoriating another the more we ought to suspect ourselves.

Now it is not a particularly inviting proposition to consider that each of us has a dark side. And the more obvious it may be to others, the less we may be open to seeing it ourselves. One divorcee, already mentioned in Chapter 1, was unmercifully harsh on her husband. At a fairly superficial level Mrs. R. had married him to reform him. This of course carried enough seeds of destruction with it. Moreover, her religiosity and moral righteousness were overbearing. From her lofty vantage point she could look down on this poor publican, her husband. She certainly thanked the Lord that she was not like him. The crowning touch in her case against her husband was the fact that he was disparaging toward her.

One might suppose that the external differences of taste and interest between this woman and her husband were real enough. What we cannot grant, though, is that she was free of the weakness and badness which she presumed characterized only her husband. Her own very weak ego-strengths were obvious. Only when she indicated that she had been in a mental hospital three different times could we appreciate how very fragile was the hold she had on reality and herself. She, in fact, was the one who wanted to be better. She was the one who felt herself slipping away. She was the one who did not have the amount of character strength she wanted.

Not everyone can look at the dark side of his own personality. Certainly Mrs. D. could not see that her own mischievous undermining of her husband was rooted in deeper strains of self-undermining which she barely warded off by putting her husband down both during the marriage and after it. At best one could wonder with her whether the possibility of her going into a bar with her husband would have been so irreligious when one remembers the accusations against Jesus of having been a friend of sinners and winebibbers. Some lessening of her self-righteous attacks upon others might modulate her inner attack upon herself. But one could not expect her to see the deeper connection between her weakness and the hostility with which she railed against the weaknesses of others. The shadow side of personality is not for all to see.

Mrs. N. had sturdier sinews. Her conviction that "no one really loves me" came from the child-self within, as we mentioned in Chapter 4. It also had the force of being her own dark side. Everyone was a "bastard" or worse in her eyes. She herself effectively chopped many to pieces. The delight and energy she poured into an attack upon someone's stupidity came from her own inner attacking powers, which not only could leap out at others but which effectively pounced upon herself. After telling a group meeting about the paralyzed state into which she would fall occasionally when she felt absolutely convinced that there was someone in her closet in the night, it was clear that the monster which she unloosed upon individuals from time to time was her own inner monster. But after what seemed like hours of paralyzed fear she would bring herself to examine the closet and check all the doors and prove to herself the hostile invader did not outwardly exist. It was this strength to fight back her own fears that let me know that Mrs. N. could stand to hear something about her own projections— not only in the dark of the night but also in the daily interaction with others.

Once one sees that there is a process by which he projects his faults onto others, he can no longer be quite so sure that his own fault-finding habits are as untainted as they once seemed. A new note of humility and even humiliation enters. And he becomes less unbearable. Even compassionate notes enter. With Mrs. N. there was one very impressive evidence of this in her reaction to religious services. In the midst of her worst period of bitterness

41

with the world, she could fasten much of the problem upon God. After all, the inadequate male she had married and divorced was a minister. She did not want to have any part in the phony baloney of religion. But as she came to grips with herself her resistance to participation in group religious services disappeared. The more she became her real self, the more she could acknowledge the reality of God in her life.

The experience of divorce when it is bitter not only hurts the ego, it upsets all one's hopes for the future. There must be a culprit. Someone else should be made to pay for the hurt and disgrace one feels. If a divorced person were capable of saying, "I am the source of my own undoing" or "I was ninety-nine percent the problem in our marriage," then I feel certain that a divorce would never have occurred in the first place. The outward pain will not go away until its inner sources have been found. The eagerness to cast stones is halted only when our own sins are acknowledged.

Mrs. K. had developed a more subtle way of not seeing her own dark side. She simply never fought back verbally or physically no matter how she felt. It became clear that she felt an enormous amount of hostility toward her husband's possessive dominance. The child-self within had quickly and thoroughly learned to turn a sweet side toward her parents no matter what she felt. She did the same thing in her marriage. Though her husband had been controlling her excessively she never fought back. Even when her Animus wandered off and found a more compassionate and companionable male, she still could not work out her feelings toward her husband. She did not want to leave him, yet here she was withdrawing from him and leaving the marriage rather than lift her voice in protest against his inconsiderateness. The removal of herself from contact with her husband meant she did not have to let the dark side of herself out. She could honestly believe that there was no bitterness or hostility *in her,* since she was not the cruel and tyrannical one. Within her, though, her anger seethed. Although she thought herself well possessed in separating from her husband, she was not. When finally she found it possible to express anger openly in counseling she made the enormous discovery of how much fight there was in herself. She fully expected her counselor to be devastated by her dark side. He wasn't. In her case some ruddy sticking-up for herself was needed in the marriage itself. A toe-to-toe struggle with the husband who childishly tried to rule her life was what she needed. Mrs. K.'s dark side seemed evil to her and therefore she had thoroughly repressed it. In fact it was not totally evil but helpful. It was just a bit of fight and spirit which her otherwise doll-like nature needed.

For Mrs. K. the evil was, again, exclusively her husband's—until she could see that there was a dark side to herself. In this instance she increased the tyrannizing tendencies of her husband by failing to check him. Put in another way, she expected to be dealt with considerately and as a princess. She looked every bit a princess. When she was not treated as one she withdrew rather than acknowledge that there were any of the hostile impulses of the commoner in her. Her withdrawal from human contact was a way of acting upon her meaner nature without seeming ill-tempered. But it did not give much opportunity for bringing things into the open. It broke contact. What she found necessary to admit was that she had more than just the surface appearance of a princess. When she did this she discovered that some of her fighting, dark side made her even more attractive. It was not nearly such a bad thing to have a few defensive feelings. But to adopt the defense that one is defenseless was a very subtle ploy to overcome. The dark side can hide some needed virtues as well as vices.

Our Western culture operates with the heavy influence of the Zoroastrian concepts of light against dark, good against evil, angels against the devil. We press for the taking of sides very early. We do not readily countenance the coexistence of the logically contrary. Thus we are more thoroughly conditioned within our culture against seeing that which contradicts and counters rather than standing loose to it. This helps us to understand why the dark side of ourselves proves so difficult to grasp either as a general concept or as an actuality within our own lives.

Yet, we who profess the Christian virtue of peace muster enormous energy for the making and "finishing" of wars. We who proclaim brotherhood systematically exclude certain groups from their full participation in the mainstream of our society. We, who squirm over the drug-taking of youth, do not see our pill-filled cupboards and the ready reliance upon distilled spirits. The problem of contraries in our lives is not limited to our individual and personal character. It infiltrates the whole of our social reality.

Let us come back then to the divorced person. My observation is that each one has a dark-side problem. This is equally true for the person still married. However, the divorced person has to examine what went wrong. And in this connection he needs to accept his own part in having made the marriage fail. But he is sorely tempted in his need to bolster himself by projecting his own faults upon his mate. To do so would not help him avoid making the next mate just as faulty as the last. The biblical path of finding oneself by losing oneself seems exceedingly pertinent here. Unless one can surrender the idealized image he holds of himself, he will not find his true self. And the true self is not just the "negative personality" but the combination of the asserted personality and the hidden darker side as well.

There is another reason to consider one's dark side and shadowy motivations. It is to a mother more urgent than the question of "finding oneself." The undetected shadow does not stop its predatory activity just because the husband has departed and is no longer in range. It casts about for other objects suitable for its projective display. And children too can be made to bear the brunt of the evil we may feel about ourselves. The son whose physical features are a constant reminder of his despised father soon finds that he cannot do much to please mother either. The daughter whose waspish behavior is peculiarly irritating may well be incorporating something from the mother which the mother does not like about herself. Woe betide the young one if the mother is not able to see it is a part of herself to which she objects! The dark side which may well be a prod to disharmony in the marriage can certainly do a lot more

44

damage in the lives of children, who are not quite so free to walk away. Through it all the mother continues her way impervious to all the harm she may be doing because she does not see her own evil intentions and actions at all.

How does one bring the projected evil back to oneself? I think it is virtually impossible unless one puts himself in a working relation with a counselor and lets a new kind of honesty be the order of the day. Certainly having other people see your evil and label it for you does not do much good. Your defenses are far too agile for so easy an undermining as that.

There is, I might add, one other glimpse of our own evil which comes to each of us regularly. Our dreams show us shadowy figures doing varying works of malice quite routinely. When one realizes that each part of the dream is a part of oneself, then the evil figures can be seen as depicting the malign purposes we have. Mrs. Z. who was coming to see me because her marriage seemed nearly useless had the following series of dreams bring her the glimpse of her own hostile and vicious impulses. The dreams centered on her mother-in-law whom Mrs. Z. perceived as an evil woman:

—In the first dream in this series, Mrs. Z. is alone with her mother-in-law and her husband. "I am positive that she is planning to kill me." In the night her suspicions are confirmed and the mother-in-law is standing over her bed with a knife. The police are called and she is carried off to an asylum.

—In a dream about a month later, Mrs. Z.'s mother-in-law invites her to luncheon and talks her into joining a Bible study group. Later she is in a horse-drawn carriage and the mother-in-law is sitting with her sister in the open back in the rain while the dreamer sits comfortably with the driver. Her mother-in-law looks angry.

—In another dream about a month later Mrs. Z. dreams that she has been given her mother-in-law's house. She dispossesses her mother-in-law without any qualms.

—A month later Mrs. Z. dreams of her mother-in-law again. This time she is in a meeting in which her mother-in-law asks all sorts of vicious little questions. Mrs. Z. tries to be patient at first, but then she answers all "her stupid questions maliciously and with hatred in my voice."

The mother-in-law in this instance is probably quite correctly perceived as someone whose respectable veneer is very thin. But what the sequence of dreams shows is a progressive movement of the evil that is perceived as being in the mother-in-law over to the point where the evil of the mother-in-law and the malicious hatred of the dreamer are one and the same. Both are engaged in malicious verbal assault upon each other in the last dream. The progression in this dream series seems to be very gentle. The unconscious is very slow in pressing the point home that the dreamer is the dreamt-of mother-in-law with all her hostile impulses. Of course an analytically trained counselor could help one see that point in the first dream. But even without a trained interpreter, one could hardly avoid the effect of the fourth dream.

The dark side of our personality is allowed to exist because the conscious person thinks "out of sight, out of mind." But this is not so. Out of sight, some forces can still be a driving part of our personality. Just because they are out of sight does not mean they do not have a say in what we do. Their influence expands in proportion to the inattention of consciousness. It contracts and comes in check through the increase of awareness. A major undertaking for any person facing difficulties in living is the tracking of his own hidden role in his difficulties. The dark side of the self is a formidable challenge to anyone.

7.

Children's
Rights

Because children are not organized into an effective force standing up for their own rights, let me voice something on their behalf.
Children have the right to two parents living together if possible.
If they cannot live together, they still have the right of access to two
parents separately. If one or the other of these adults is a scoundrel,
they have the additional right of finding this out for themselves and
making up their own minds about it.

It is tempting, since they are so young and vulnerable, to use
the right of being their mother as the avenue for extending venomous
feelings toward the former husband. It usually is the case that the
mother and children stay together. The father is excluded from the
daily circle. This opens the door to letting the children know the
mother's attitude toward her former husband. In the tug-of-war the
children are the rope which is stretched and pulled mercilessly as
they are handed back and forth for visits.

There is little reason to suppose that two people who found
it impossible to live together should suddenly find it in their hearts
to be charitable toward one another. In some rare instances, of course,
divorces are genuine mutual agreements in which both principals are
convinced that they are better separated than together. But usually
there is a sea of recriminations and bitterness between them. It seems

unusually difficult to ask a divorced mother to start taking a benign and neutral attitude toward the children's father and vice versa.

But perhaps one of the rights of children is that the fighting and difficulty between their parents should cease when the parents admit they cannot live together. Yet, the most obvious way in which the mother can extend the battle lines without appearing to be hostile is to be difficult about the visiting times with the father.

The mother who has not been reticent in finding fault with the father while he was a husband will usually be adept in finding reasons why the separated or divorced father will not be a good influence on her children. One woman described her husband as immature, impulsive, interested in hotrods, golf, cards, the boys, and sex when he wants it. She was sure that he would be an evil influence upon their eight-year-old daughter. Perhaps he would. But the child needs to be given access to the father, if the father is willing to see her, and a chance to make up her own mind about the father. So long as the father is interested in visits with his children, the children stand to benefit from the knowledge that they are valued by both a mother and a father.

To be sure, the visitations of the children with a divorced father may be more like an uncle or grandparent's visit. Many fathers plan the visit time as fun and games for the brief period they are together with their children. Some make it a time of adding gifts and toys, which makes them a perpetual Santa Claus. But the mother needs to ignore the superficial and remember that the children deserve the feeling that they are loved by each parent.

In time the children will make their own assessment of what the feeling and love contribution of each parent has been. They may change their minds several times during the developing years because of the conflict between their parents. Eventually, though, they will recognize love if it has been present. This they will value above all else. It is little enough for them to gain — given the chagrin they will feel over their parents' failure. But if a man is a good father to your children even though he has not been a good husband, do not spoil the values that he can contribute still to your children.

One of the places where inner conflict can rise within the mother who is bitter about her husband's departure is at the point of visiting times and vacations. One woman who felt quite capable of being "mature" in her decisions, and who knew she wanted to do what was best for the children, kept finding the old animosities aroused every time her husband asked for some variation in the visiting times or the vacation division. She kept suspecting that her husband was only putting on a show for his new wife (the third marriage for him) because he had never bothered during their marriage (his second) to visit with the children of his first marriage. The fact was that he was determined to maintain his fatherly love and affection for the children of his second marriage because he now saw with twenty years' hindsight how bitter the sons of his first marriage felt over having been forgotten and abandoned by their father. To her credit, it must be said that the second divorced wife phoned for a counseling appointment every time she felt her reactions to her former husband's plans were strong. She knew that something was still churning inside herself regarding her own marriage's failure and she was afraid that this could easily spoil her own relationship to her three daughters. One of the more helpful meetings which occurred among a series that took place about every three months was a three-way conference between the former husband, the divorced wife, and myself.

This conference cleared the air immensely. Feelings of hurt and rejection and anger which stretched back into the marriage itself were expressed by both former partners. With a third party present, they were able to ventilate these feelings without having them get out of hand. It was quite clear that the distress over the mechanics of the husband's visits and vacation plans was a cover-up for the preservation of old hurts.

Not too surprisingly most parents want to do the right thing for their children even if their own marriage does not work out. One of the matters they may overlook, though, is the amount of distress and confusion the child or children may feel over their parents' marital failure. When the reasons for the breakup are not obvious, the children, especially younger ones, will plead mercilessly for a resumption of things as they were. Letting children have the chance to get their own feelings out is another right they should be accorded. If the mother cannot talk with the children freely so that their hurts and grief in the loss of father's presence are heard, then she may want to open doors so that a school counselor or teacher helps at this point. A close friend can be enough. Formal appointments with a professional counselor or psychologist may be too much unless there are several indications of behavior you cannot understand. By too much I mean only to caution parents against making it seem as though your children are a psychiatric problem. If you yourself are intensively seeking counseling help, then your children will benefit. There is little benefit for children sent to counselors as scapegoats for their parents' problems.

This brings me to another right of children in the midst of a divorce crisis. They have a right to a healthier parent. A healthier parent is one who has faced the problems of his own failure and difficulty in the marriage that ended. A healthier mother, for example, is one who is open to acknowledging her true feelings and does not need to hide them either from herself or from others. A healthier parent is a mother who has struggled to gain a new kind of honesty with herself — so that she has both a new awareness of herself and an awareness of her children as real persons with feelings and views of their own.

Children have great abilities to be insightful and understanding. But they have the right not to be made a therapist for the parent. I am aware of one tragic circumstance in which the mother has found her oldest child immensely wise and understanding from about age five on. During many of the years to follow, this daughter was the calm center of a very neurotic household. When the marriage broke up after fifteen hectic years, her mother gained her therapeutic help from her marvelously open teen-age daughter. But that teen-ager has been robbed of her own parent in the process of the parent's use of her for the kind of discussion which should have proceeded with a counselor. The rights of children to a healthy parent then has a corollary — the right not to have to give up their own healthiness by being called to be emotionally supporting to a parent.

The child who ought not be pressed into the role of the therapist of the remaining parent, ought also not to have to be the substitute for the departed parent. Mothers who can easily project onto sons much of what was wrong with their former husbands can equally mistreat those sons by making them take the emotional place of their fathers. This happens so often that it is, I fear, the greatest single oppressive consequence of divorce. There is enough natural coalescence between mothers and sons not to be adding to it. Yet the removal of the father adds fuel to the fire. Some of the fuel comes from the irrational depths both of the child and of the mother. A divorced mother who has growing sons or teen-age sons needs to take with added seriousness the pleas made throughout this book to "hie thee to a counselor." The son has a right to a mother, not a lover. Not until it is clear to the son that his mother is not depending upon him emotionally will he be able to reckon with the fact that maybe she does not secretly need him. The mother cannot make this clear without gaining a good deal of self-understanding.

8.

The
One Who
Understands

The matters we have touched upon so far have been the matters which you will discover in counseling when marriage ends. There are countless other concerns which numerous other books discuss. In *Parents Without Partners*[1] you will learn about the social groups that have been formed by persons having similar problems of going it alone with children after a divorce or death. In Morton Hunt's *The World of the Formerly Married*,[2] you will find the prospects of new companionship and remarriage discussed with a lively zest. In William J. Goode's *Women in Divorce*,[3] you will find the sociologist's statistics regarding all kinds of questions about the people who undergo divorce, the problems they face, the outcomes of the experience. In *The Divorcee's Handbook*,[4] you will find a direct discussion of most of the problems faced in divorce adjustments. And there are several first-person accounts by divorcees.

1. Jim and Janet Egleson, *Parents Without Partners* (New York: Ace Books, 1961).
2. Morton M. Hunt, *The World of the Formerly Married* (New York: McGraw-Hill, 1966).
3. William J. Goode, *Women in Divorce* (New York: Free Press, 1965).
4. Louise Rohner, *The Divorcee's Handbook* (Garden City, N.Y.: Doubleday, 1967).

The assumption of this writer is that your reading should lead you to a counselor, to one who understands. Each of the topics discussed to this point is meant to suggest aspects of what you would be likely to talk over in the months or years of seeing a trained counselor. There remains the necessity of mentioning one more problem and this is a problem which arises by virtue of seeking counseling.

You perhaps can anticipate it from the chapter title. In numerous ways the evidence points to one overwhelming wish regarding the kind of person one would like in marriage — one who understands. If you are churned up because of the breakdown of communication which occurred in your marriage and are turning to a counselor who is professionally trained to be understanding, then somewhere during your visits you are apt to imagine (if he is a male) that your counselor would make the perfect partner. If this happens you would not be the first to cut that groove.

So fundamental is this phenomenon that the early depth psychologists — Freud, Jung, and others — quickly saw it. They described it as "transference." While the transference may take on hostile forms, as it frequently did in my work with Mrs. N., its most typical form is positive. One finds that one's affectionate feelings toward a parent out of a long-past childhood are rekindled by talking about oneself openly with an understanding listener.

The hostile transference arises when the original parent was a rejecting or thoroughly inadequate figure. The child who learned to expect hatred or disregard from the Significant Other person carries this expectancy with him all the time. In a counseling relationship, the counselor becomes the Significant Other from whom one anticipates malicious acts. In a closing group session of one single-parent-family camp week, I asked each person to write a brief word of advice to someone in comparable circumstances. I indicated I might use their statements in this book. Everyone but Mrs. N. joined in the invitation. What came forth for the most part were urgings to seek "expert help." Since this is the one clear stress throughout this book, it was not something I felt needed to be added. However, the reply of Mrs. N. revealed the strong hostility she was prepared to feel whenever her "father" asked her to do something: "I don't feel like helping you write your book." Knowing all the "people-are-no-good" feelings she had from being rejected and abused as a child, I could quickly accept this as a "transference" of feelings she felt in her childhood toward her father and mother. The negative transference dissipates when the counselor provides a new set of reactions to the old hostility by not becoming hostile himself.

The positive transference revolves around all the infantile wishes that one could have the understanding parent all to oneself. It takes the form of "we could make such beautiful music together." If the counselor is untrained, inexperienced, or in personal conflict, he will mistake the overtures and entreaties as personal. There have been just enough instances of clergy and others getting a divorce and marrying someone they had been counseling for one to recognize that transference reactions are very powerful and very flattering if one is not sensitive to what lies back of them. Back of them in a woman is a wandering Animus which is projecting upon a male counselor all sorts of things that she wants. When the counselor is not familiar with his own Anima, he too can project it onto a suitable counselee. When both projections are working, the mix is overwhelming in its force. As we indicated earlier, in Chapter 5, the projections of the Animus and the Anima may be enough to connect two people but there is a lot more of reality to each person which needs to be seen as well.

The transference reaction is hardly avoidable in intensive counseling work. Even where a counselor and a counselee decide not to work together, the underlying reasons usually include some mutual negative transference issue. When counselor and counselee want to work together there is usually some element of mutual positive transference.

The difference between a skilled counselor and an unskilled one revolves around the counselor's own training and learning about himself through his own analysis. The depth psychologists insisted from the beginning of their movement that the person who wishes to help another person in the sphere of inner reactions must become acquainted with his own inner complexes. He needs to know when he is vulnerable to the appeal of what kind of person so that he need not simply fall into the bear-traps that positive transference needs set. Because even the best of counselors will find that their childhood complexes may be triggered by counselees, as a result of their own analytic training they guard against their countertransference reaction. At the point where the counselor feels himself being attracted to his counselee, he should know what is happening and how to keep himself from getting in the way of the counselee's constructive movement beyond the transference.

Classical psychoanalysis even goes so far as to take the transference phenomenon as the heart of psychoanalytic work. The psychoanalyst willingly creates a transference problem. He has the patient project upon him the inappropriate typical responses he makes to others which get the patient into unhappy binds. Then he helps the person to analyze the "transference neurosis" as a way of showing the patient how to escape the neurotic patterns he pursues outside the psychoanalyst's office.

It is far better that the first person who rekindles a loving flame within after a broken marriage be the person helping you rather than the first person who comes along. The possibility of just being on the rebound if matters are left to chance is high. The prospect changes if you begin to work through all of the confusions which led you into and out of marriage.

The chief work of your postmarital life is reordering your own life. It is time-consuming. It can be costly too, although there are many resources of clergy and community agencies which do not depend upon the usual fee-for-service relationship. Its greatest costs are in emotional terms. Trying to be honest with yourself is a very difficult undertaking. Finding that there are hurt feelings, issues of bereavement, residuals of childhood, actions of an unknown inner partner, and devious activities of your dark side may astonish and annoy you. Eventually each of these discoveries can add to the confidence you need for meeting and facing life. Each of these facets of personality when discovered and accepted moves you along toward the wholeness of your own person. That resultant will be different from any image of adequacy you might have held, but it will be far more workable, resilient, and reliable than any fantasy creation.

Carl G. Jung in a concluding remark on a BBC-filmed interview suggested that if we go with nature we will be all right. What he had in mind as "nature" is not just the impulses of desire, but the diverse elements of our own inner world which are, after all, a part of the nature we humans have. When you find a person who understands and is willing to help you find the varied facets of your own nature, more than just a projection of the Anima or the Animus takes place. There is a lasting appreciation for the person who helps you to become more of a real person. The counselor's rewards are in seeing this happen.